Second-hand clothes

The ACE project
'Literacy for active citizenship' series

Written by Dorothy Glynn
Illustrations by Hugo Dudley

Second-hand clothes
© Learning Unlimited 2014

Published by Learning Unlimited Ltd as part of the Active
Citizenship and Literacy (ACE) project. The ACE project led by
Learning Unlimited, was funded through the European Integration
Fund and delivered in partnership with Blackfriars Settlement,
Working Men's College and the Institute of Education.

Foreword

The ACE project
'Literacy for active citizenship' series

The Active Citizenship and English (ACE) project, led by Learning Unlimited and delivered in partnership with Blackfriars Settlement, Working Men's College and the Institute of Education, received funding from the European Integration Fund (July 2013 to June 2015).

The ACE project aimed to support non-EU women to develop their skills and confidence in English as well as the knowledge and confidence to take an active part in everyday life in the UK. As part of the project we wanted to produce a series of readers for our learners, and other adults also settling in the UK, which include stories about funny, personal and less typical aspects of everyday life in the UK. These books were written by learners and volunteers on the ACE project and the supporting activities have been developed by the Learning Unlimited team.

We hope you enjoy using the 'Literacy for active citizenship' series.

To find out more about the ACE project, please see: **www.learningunlimited.co/projects/ace**

Second-hand shops, vintage shops
and charity shops are very popular
in the UK.

In charity shops you can buy nearly-new clothes for very low prices. For example, I recently bought a pair of jeans for 70p.

Charity shops can be very good for people who don't have a lot of money. The money the shops make goes to charities such as *Oxfam, Cancer Research* or the *British Heart Foundation*

Second-hand shops sell lots of different things such as books, clothes and furniture. Some people buy second-hand clothes because they are cheap or a lot cheaper than ordinary shops. The money from these shops does not go to charities.

Vintage shops are different to charity shops. They are second-hand shops that specialise in clothes and items from the past. For example, some vintage shops only sell clothes from the 1940s, 50s or 60s. A lot of people are very interested in the fashion and music of these times.

My nephew, Paul, likes buying 1940s American clothes from vintage shops. He recently found a very rare Pea coat. He was very happy, especially because it was not very expensive.

This is how Paul describes his Pea coat:

"This is a United States Navy Pea coat. It is navy blue and it has two rows of buttons and vertical pockets.

The number of buttons on a Pea coat tells us when it was made. This coat has 10 buttons and each one has a picture of an anchor. This means it was made in the 1940s.

You can see the name of the original owner on the lining. This is a very special vintage coat."

Key words

anchor	a heavy piece of metal at the end of a chain or rope to stop a boat from moving in water
charity shops	shops that give the money they make to a charity, for example: *Oxfam*. People give things to a charity shop so that the shops can sell them and give the money to charity.
lining	material inside a dress or coat that is different to the main material on the outside
Navy	the sea army
navy blue	dark blue
nephew	the son of your brother or sister

owner	the person that something belongs to, for example: *I am the owner of that car, it is mine.*
passionate	really like something, for example: *My son is passionate about football*
popular	something that many people like, for example: *X Factor is a very popular tv programme*
second-hand shops	shops that sell things that someone else has already used
vertical	go straight up
vintage shops	shops that sell things from certain times in the past such as the 1950s

Questions

1. Why do people like charity shops?

2. What did Paul buy?

3. Why was he happy?

4. Do you know anyone who likes clothes from the 1940s, 50s or 60s?

5. Do you buy second-hand clothes?

6. Do you like charity shops?

7. In your country, are there shops that sell second-hand clothes?

8. What do you do with your old clothes?

Activities

1. Use the internet. Find pictures of clothes from the 1940s, 1950s and 1960s.

2. In pairs, talk about the clothes you find:
   - Which clothes do you like?
   - Describe the colour, length and shape of the clothes.
   - Are they different to clothes now? How?

For more downloadable activities, visit:
www.learningunlimited.co/resources/publications

Acknowledgements

Second-hand clothes was written by Dorothy Glynn and illustrated by Hugo Dudley. We are grateful to them for being able to include their work as part of the 'Literacy for active citizenship' series.

To find out more about Learning Unlimited, its resources and published materials, CPD and teacher training programmes, project and consultancy work, please see: **www.learningunlimited.co**